RIPPLES

ALSO BY
AHREND TORREY

Bird City, American Eye

Small Blue Harbor

RIPPLES

POEMS BY

AHREND TORREY

PINYON PUBLISHING
Montrose, Colorado

Cover Art "School of Fish Are Swimming on the Night Sky" by ToBeeLife

Photograph of Ahrend Torrey by Jonathan Dacula
Pensacola Beach, Florida

First Edition: February 2023

Pinyon Publishing
23847 V66 Trail, Montrose, CO 81403
www.pinyon-publishing.com

Library of Congress Control Number: 2022950887
ISBN: 978-1-936671-90-8

ACKNOWLEDGMENTS

Thank you to all of the editors at the following journals for first publishing some of the poems in this collection, though sometimes in earlier versions.

Amethyst Review, "Holy Basil"

North Dakota Quarterly, "Caution," "Southern Living," and "The Pink Petunia"

Pinyon Review, "The Monarchs are Dying"

Plum Tree Tavern, "Ripples"

2River, "Now that It's as Cold as It Gets"

Saint Katherine Review, "Light," "Polar Bear, Starving," and "Carolina Wren"

Sisyphus Magazine, "Mockingbirds"

Snarl, "Exceptions" and "Think of This"

The Black Fork Review, "Mental Illness of a Gay Boy," "Southern-Faggot Blues," and "What We Do with Extinction"

The Curator, "What Fear Can Do"

The Perch, a creative arts journal of the Yale Program for Recovery and Community Health, a program of the Yale School of Medicine, "How the Pandemic Killed Me"

The Westchester Review, "Field Crickets"

Welter Online, "Still,"

West Trade Review, "Watery Dazzling Dialectic (or A Gender Proem)"

Thank you to all of the past and present poets who teach
and guide me along the way—Langston Hughes, Ruth Stone,
Linda Gregg, Mary Oliver, Jack Gilbert, Jim Harrison,
Etheridge Knight, Cavafy, Natasha Trethewey, Kim Addonizio,
Mark Doty, Elizabeth Bishop, William Carlos Williams,
James Wright, Mark Strand, Anne Sexton, Gwendolyn Brooks,
Walt Whitman, Raymond Carver, Li-Young Lee, Ada Limón,
Frank O'Hara, Philip Larkin, Marie Howe, Carl Sandburg,
William Stafford, Yusef Komunyakaa, Jane Kenyon,
and many others.

Thank you to Susan Entsminger, my editor at Pinyon
Publishing, for your dedication, guidance, friendship, and for
your kind and glowing spirit.

Thank you to J. Marcus Weekley for giving this manuscript
a quick read, right before publication, and on a time crunch.
Thank you too for our awesome, lasting friendship.

Thank you to life, Nature, my friends, and to my animals
Dichter, Dova, and Purl.

Thank you to my wonderful husband, Jonathan, with whose
love and support these words were written. I am so thankful
for our life together. Also, thank you for helping me copyedit
this collection before publication.

And yes, thank you reader—thank you, thank you.

For Jonathan, my light, my light—

A subtle chain of countless rings;
The next unto the farthest brings…

—*Ralph Waldo Emerson*

Contents

I. THINK OF THIS

II. TWENTY-TWENTY

III. AMERICA IN THE TWENTY-FIRST CENTURY

IV. HOW CULTURE DAMNS

Note

In this collection, I often use "they," "them," and "their,"
as third-person singular nonbinary pronouns.

—A.

I.

Think of This

IT'S PITCH-NIGHT

and from a crack in the curtains,

I see a sliver of light, spray
from the neighbor's back porch—

all the way to my resting
                    hand.

How brilliant, you sliver of light, I see.
How remarkable, in all the night.
How impactful, you sliver of light, I see—

you one, disregarded, sliver.

EXCEPTIONS

I wake from deep sleep.
I can't fall back to dream,
therefore, I lift my body
and hobble
      to the kitchen
      to make coffee.

There's nothing greater about morning
than the cat curled
in my lap.
Except

for the way she *hums*—
Except

for the way she kneads at the blanket over my leg—
Except

for the way she sleeps when I step to the patio—
Except

for the sun lifting itself, over the fence, and the tree—
Except

for the scent of mildew, and freshly mown grass—
Except

for the sudden towhee—
Except,
except,
except—

Your turn now.

CAROLINA WREN

Had you slept-in this quiet Monday,
   you wouldn't have heard it.

Had you gone to the grocery,
   you wouldn't have heard it—

this Carolina Wren's
   cheery-cheery-cheery.

This Carolina Wren, only you hear,
   quick-singing, its singular song…

THINK OF THIS

If you move your mug
    to a different spot on the patio table,
everything on Earth shifts—

air shifts, dust shifts:
perhaps a bird on a branch sneezes and
    the branch shakes,

                a leaf falls.

Weeds underneath lighten yellow
    and hold moisture for purslane seed
to absorb—and burst orange! white! pink!

Every motion, no matter how small,
    consider it
        deeply.

How drastically the air—
    when we rush by—moves the Earth—

RIPPLES

A pine nut falls into the dark, still pond—

a ripple-wave appears, then another

ripple-wave appears, then another

ripple-wave appears, then another

ripple-wave appears, then another

pine nut falls into the dark, still pond...

PURL, AND THE MOSQUITO

When I choose not to pick Purl up from the beige rug in the kitchen
that we use to hide the cracked tile, I find it intriguing
that I've not altered her future. Now, she sneaks to the storm door
to pounce a mosquito bumping the glass. With her paw, she eats it.

Had I picked her up, pushed my face into the thick black fur of her neck
—to love her—the mosquito might live another day, siphoning the blood
of something else, maybe, some dog, even: giving it those fatal heartworms,
perhaps.

NOW THAT IT'S AS COLD AS IT GETS

in the Deep South, think how the dead doe hangs
from the hunters' tailgate—
head, bobbing, down the highway…

When they get her home, hang her up
from rafters in the shed, they won't understand
as blood drips from her pale tongue and pools
at their feet. But as they pull /and pull /and pull
—they'll soon find out—

just how badly she wants to keep   her skin.

DECEMBER

The Titmouse makes that sound again:
peter-peter-peter.

Sitting outside my house,
in a maple, on the edge of the birdbath, perhaps,
making that sound again:
peter-peter-peter-peter.

Inside, I close my eyes,
feel the air conditioner, tickle my bare arm—
each chill rising like a meerkat
to see what is happening.

The Titmouse
perched beyond these walls,
outside my house again,
makes that sound again:
peter-peter-peter-peter.

Because this December day is like three pastel tulips:

    Peter-peter-peter—

    Peter-peter-peter—

    Peter-peter-peter.

OUT THE WINDOW

squirrels swing around the myrtle tree;
acrobats
       hanging
from branch
            to chain
from chain
       to grain
in the feeder.

They sling around their duster-tails,

 jump

      down—
      then-back-up-the-trunk.

They dangle at Purl, my cat,
while her silhouette watches front row.

She glares beyond her reflection—
quivers her tail.

  She stoops low.
  She stoops low.

WHAT FEAR CAN DO

The plump squirrel out the corner of my eye,
    winds very near to me, within arm's reach.
I should be honored. I should stretch up
my cracked hand
  and let it crawl down and bless my body.

  I'm frightened at its sudden appearance,
   at the clump of gray fur moving
    ever so slightly toward me.
So I jump, and it jumps,
  yet unhurried
   as if its work with me is incomplete.

  It winds its gray body slowly
   back around the slick myrtle branch—
then over the faded rooftop—

  then on to bless some other matter
  of Earth—

THE MONARCHS ARE DYING

We hurry, hurry—

The monarchs are dying.

We hurry, hurry—

The monarchs are dying.

We hurry, hurry—

to the bar, the grocery,
the bank, the carwash,
the cookout, the casino,
the parade, the party...

The monarchs are dying.
The monarchs are dying.

Scientists estimate the monarch population in the eastern U.S. has fallen about 80% since the mid-1990s, while the drop-off in the western U.S. has been even steeper.

—*USA Today,* Dec, Fifteenth, Twenty-Twenty

A SONG INTO THE OPEN AIR

How grand you are Appalachia Mountains,
among the oldest of your kind, world of your own,
green and obscure.

Your stones will survive us, survive us.

And you Grand Canyon, with your deep crevices,
split open like melon
in summer.

Your red soil will survive us, survive us.

We are shredding Earth, like dozers
we digest Earth, like toads
we piss over Her face
gasping and gasping

like drowning
at sea.

Oh sea, oh *life-giving* sea,
you too will survive us—

survive us, survive us.

JUMPING MULLET,
IN THE COIN AGE

I gaze from the water's edge, far into the blue—

Like silver coins flinging into the air—
mullet fly and flop—everywhere!

Has luck struck me?

Have I hit the lottery?

(Go ahead, laugh.)

At last, at last—I'm wealthy!

WHAT WE DO WITH EXTINCTION

All the worms have disappeared.

Robins, with their gray wings and orange breast,
eat bits of glass, then harden to crystal.

Years later, we find one in a ditch
glistening like a block of ice in a congested neighborhood.

We say: *"Oh, oh—what a lovely, lovely*

  centerpiece!"

OMIT

Sentimentality, okay.
I get cliché.

But birds? Omit birds??

—I don't get birds.

MOCKINGBIRDS

Today I see the Myrtle tree, the lone Myrtle tree,
    the vibrant Myrtle tree, and across the yard a Chinese tallow
        losing a branch, crackling to the ground,
    not tomorrow, but today.

In the wind I hear the trees, the boastfulness of the trees,
    the hiss like a snake; they say, *I too belong here, should*
    root here, should be angry today, but not tomorrow.

    Gray Squirrel outlines the eaves of the house,
        grass is aglow with native flowers,
            today, but not tomorrow, Summer is ablaze,
                gulls float above Lake Pontchartrain, Mars is an orange
        speck, in the night sky.

Not tomorrow, but today, through smog in
    California and New York City, factories
        surrounding Beijing, through forests falling in Malaysia
        and Indonesia, and waves of plastic, bottles, bags
    washing ashore.

    Through the oily waters of the Mississippi, roadkill,
        destroyed habitats and broken ecosystems of the South,
        today, not tomorrow, but today, out the back patio
        mockingbirds chase each other—
        through the hollies!

ARE YOU AWARE?

Are you aware
the wind
makes the tall palm
crackle like a sack?

High up it crackles
like a popping
wood flame,
or like a flapping old flag.

Are you aware
when you close your eyes
that gust
makes the tall palm hiss
like hard rain, hiss
like hard rain?

Are you aware
air can make a palm
do anything?

TRANSCENDING,
LATE SPRING

yesss, yesss, yesss,
          say the trees—
yesss, yesss, yesss—

yesss, yesss, yesss,
          say the trees—

POLAR BEAR, STARVING

Some people talk to animals.
Not many listen though.

—A.A. Milne

You won't see them in your business suit.
You won't see them on your grocery run.
You won't see them on your Sunday morning stroll
across the Causeway bridge,
like white sailing gulls flapping the sky.

Go north for miles and miles—
cross the Hudson Bay.
After several long days you'll reach them
in the Arctic.

You'll spot them on dripping ice.
Scrounging like giant strays.
Thin and filled with worms.
Skin sucked to their bones.
Pus settled at the corner of their eyes
like dried lemon curd.

Look at the muddy raged one
with the skeleton's face—
how it slow-stands on hind legs
like a sick hare.

What's it roaring? You ask.
Are we too far to hear?
Thin breath; hard glare.
What's it roaring, roaring?—

LIGHT

Where do we go from here?
Where do we turn? I say stay
and watch the hummingbird buzz the air.
I suppose it knows where it's going,
though we don't. Over the rooftops,
it's content, focused
—a stream of light.

Maybe it is Light, that Thing bigger than us.
Maybe It's not unseen; maybe It's in front
of our eyes; maybe It's where we sit
at the kitchen table, and look through the window,
one arm propped on the other, next to the orchid.

Maybe it's Light, too, that still green thing.

Or maybe It's a different scene: the sugar ant
crawling the wall, then up the mirror,

or the stubborn fly knocking the screen,
knock-knocking the screen, the screen

—trying to get in.

STILL,

the heat rises. Still,
  factories smolder. Still,
    oil rigs pump their black vomit
      through our veins. Still,
        the lion is an erased sketch—
          the willow, a question.

If these years pass,
  and oil rigs are no longer a thing,
    if plastic, is no longer a thing,
      I assure you have something,
        as grim, as hopeless. Still,

the Mississippi rushes forward—
  looking for a turn. Still,
    you can write the word *Maybe*. Still,
      the sun pulls herself
        out of the dark lake, vibrant,
          as if nothing, absolutely nothing,
            can stop her—

HOLY BASIL

I notice the young holy basil,
delicate,

with its two shiny leaves
like tiny elephant ears.

I ask it, why we live—
then leave it for a day
and come back.

Then leave it for a day
and come back.

Without directly answering the question:

each day
I watch it *grow*.

ANOTHER REASON I LISTEN

My husband is deep asleep on the sofa.
Our cat, Purl, in her dark place,

just under the corner of our bed,
is balled behind the bed skirt.

I clank through the house,
not thinking of noise. I steep tulsi.

Until I hear faintly
as the drawer-squeak,

> —*"There's not just you,
> there's us"*—

am I mindful
of the others.

II.
Twenty-Twenty

DURING THE PANDEMIC, ON THE BACK PATIO

The sun blazes—
all the while
many choke on ventilators,
like each house in this neighborhood
choked to electricity, wires drape
pole to pole,
drooping down the throat
of each home.

Thousands drown
like weights chained to their ankles,
like they've been pushed—
into the Chandeleur Sound.

They've almost given up. The healthcare workers,
assembled like ships of sailors
trying to lift the dying, pound by pound.

But the dying are too heavy, too many.
By the time one is saved, hundreds gasp
then burble
        down.

All the while the sun blazes,
and the wrens go on ripping—
through the somberness, abound…

AT THE BEGINNING OF COVID, I SHOP

I pick up a box of rigatoni.
I do not touch my face.
A gallon of 2%.
I do not touch my face.
Two cans of chicken broth.
I do not touch my face.

I scan at the checkout.
Damn, I need to itch my face!

I drive all the way home.
I do not scratch my face.
I unload the car.
I do not scratch my face.
I put away the groceries.
I do not scratch my face.

I scrub my hands for twenty seconds—

watch mud
twirl down
the drain.

I dry my hands with soft towel.
Damn—I itch my face!

WERE YOU SOME KIND OF GOD?

When I was sick, hacking
thick mucus from my lungs,
weak and wrapped in bed
for days, I looked up to you,
with your hand extending

down to me, a bottle of
water. You said, *Here—drink.*

HOW THE PANDEMIC KILLED ME

Top U.S. Officials Warn of 'Our Pearl Harbor';
Deaths in Country May be Undercounted
—New York Times *Headline*
April Fifth, Twenty-Twenty

Too many lives taken—
I say to myself—
too many lives.

So I touch the petunia out of hope it can save us,

nothing.

I let the big ear of the geranium
run through my hand,

nothing.

I clip the stalk of the rust-colored daylily,

nothing.

I'm so gone,
I poke my finger at the long-thorned cactus:
it bleeds…

Nothing. I feel nothing.

Nothing.

EASIER SAID THAN DONE

No matter how much they try,
the sheets of clouds can never
put out the resplendent sun.

Like a god shining out
from the darks of the universe—
the orange beams and beams and beams—
over all the Earth.

Pelicans can't snuff it,
nor can jets, snuff it,
nor can the thick mossy oaks
snuff it.

No matter how many loved ones pass,
no matter how many difficulties come,

something is here
telling us that we can go on,
like everything—

like the sun
goes on—

like the river
goes on—

like the thrush
goes on—

CAUTION

thank you, Jonathan

This mentality—*if it's not affecting me,*
it's no big deal—is a virus in and of itself,

that will somehow make its way
to someone's cousin, or mother,

someone's friend, or brother,
someone's sister, or father,

until we all lie back-flat in the middle
of our yards, without a single breath,

and flies lap around our feet,
our swollen hips, our breastbone...

TWENTY-TWENTY

My sunglasses   /are broken.

     The decorative mallard
     on the front porch,

where the tip of the weed-eater nicked
     its bill

     /is broken.

The healthcare system   /broken.

     The ignition coil   /broken.

This is no exaggeration,
so much   /is broken—

     I'm   /broken.

The family   /broken.

     America   /broken—

shattered—

like a glass

         thrown—

to   the

floor.

FRUSTRATION, AFTER READING A NEWS ARTICLE

Oh, Southern Evangelicals—
how can the COVID vaccine be
"the mark of the beast,"
when those who haven't gotten the shot,
are hacking-over, dead, in hospitals?

What a sick God you must have
feverishly infecting "His own."

STORY OF THE CONEFLOWERS

A bro pulls into the drive.

He spooks a finch into the pine bough
      where it shits—
               in a lady's flowerpot:

Coneflowers shoot into blossom. Late spring
she grabs her kitchen-scissors,
then cuts them
like a cord. She drops the stems
    into a glass vase

on her sick friend's shelf in the hospital.
      An intern knocks them over—

          white!   pink!
            yellow!—

with their elbow...

THE TELLING OF A CENTRAL THEME

What I do, or don't do, directly, or indirectly, affects you.
What you do, or don't do, directly, or indirectly, affects me.

What they do, or don't do, directly, or indirectly, affects us.
What we do, or don't do, directly, or indirectly, affects them.

And this is the way of life.
And this is why it matters.

III.

America in the
Twenty-First Century

WHY I WANT TO MOVE
FROM THE NORTH SHORE

Leaving the grocery,
rolls an everyday occurrence:
a dude in a GMC truck, throws out middle finger—
slow car pulling in front of him.

—He revs his engine.—

I read white text next to a confederate flag
on his back window, tinted:

"If I offend you, I'm sorry…

you're a little BITCH!"

GEORGE FLOYD
OR BLACK IN AMERICA

/I. /Can't. /Bree

/th————————————————————————

WHITE MAN

"If I die,
I better die on an even-number day.

I see the names,
and nothing pisses me off more
than to think I could die
on a day that's not the Lord's.

Talking about the Lord's Day,
forget summer and all its fried-up leaves,
winter when every yard has gone to shit;
I better die in spring!

If I die, goddammit, if I die,
it better be the nicest day on Earth,

or dammit—you better bet—
you all will pay for it!"

AMERICA IN THE
TWENTY-FIRST CENTURY

is trying to remember those
in-between

this black-

and-white, world.

WHEN THE MAN THREW OUT HIS SOUL

When the man threw out his soul, he bought a Lamborghini.

He bought a flashy boat and cruised it on the weekends
hoping people onshore would see it.

He forgot everything that matters
and bought a four-story house and a private island, far in the Gulf,
and invited all his acquaintances to brag about his sirloin
and caviar.

For years he did this: he bought, and bought, and bought

   —then abruptly as a plane-
      bang!

  was left with nothing.

WATERY DAZZLING DIALECTIC
(OR A GENDER PROEM)

inspired by Elizabeth Bishop's "Santarém"

Look at those two rivers, those two rivers that Elizabeth overlooked while she lived in Santarém. Not the sky, of gorgeous under-lit clouds she saw. But the rivers, where the green-blue river meets the muddy river—muddy-brown like the Mississippi. It's the Tapajós merging with the Amazon. Look at the meeting of the two, closely; more closely than you've ever looked. Stoop down in the boat. Kneel on your knees in the boat. Lean over the edge at the very touching of the two—where the seagulls shimmer off the water— where sun glimmers. Push down your palms at the very line, then scoop them up: the two distinctly colored waters. What do you see now, cupped in your palms? Not the dense brown, like first you saw, not the green-blue, but another color, another color.

CHILDREN AREN'T ASSIGNED A GENDER

The children in this world
aren't assigned a gender:

Skyler,
with a vagina,
has short green hair.
They're fascinated
with soccer.

People refer to Skyler
as *he,* and *her.*

Finley,
with a penis,
has long pink hair.
They have a thing for dance
and dress-up.

People refer to Finley
as *her,* and *him.*

They grow up choosing:
their life—

WHEN I SAID

the deep clouds of the storm
waned into the morning light,

and a welder took son to lake,
sat on lakefront wall, ate beignets,

licked powdered sugar fingers, pointed
at great blue heron—

did you think *man, man, man,*
when I said "welder"? If so,

what happened to *Woman*?

BOYS

Think about those two boys
(who identify as boys)
 from Mandeville.

Think if one, you pick which one,
begs the other to go canoeing
from the north side of the lake,
to the south.

If after much kissing, and their feet
dangle touching at the old wooden pier
—they decide to go!

Think if the boat flips five miles out;
if both frantically flail and panic
for the breath of the other.

Think of the sounds as they gasp
and breathe in water, their shouts—

      gurgling
         under…

      gurgling
         under…

Think if there was some buoy nearby.
Think if they were taught how to swim.

THEY

rap to a passenger side window,

take one glance at me, then stop.

The light turns green,
then they continue on—

     rat-a-tat-
     tatting...

ON LIVING *IN* THE DEEP SOUTH

Like a promise never kept, the myrtle tree sits
in someone's lawn on the lakefront, resting
patiently in a pot. Days pass, weeks,
months, and now the myrtle is stuck
neglected for years. Oh, don't hate me—
but it's been reaching its roots through the pot,
which has stunted its growth, from ever fully
making it out.

RELIGIOUS TRAUMA

You're going
to fucking hell!
You're going
to fucking hell!
You're going
to fucking hell!
You're going
to fucking hell!
You're going
to fucking hell!
You're going
to fucking hell!
You're going
to fucking hell!

THERAPY IN A SMALL TOWN

I'm gay. *Let's pray for you, let's pray.*

I'm gay. *You can wash it away.*

I'm anxious. *It's because you're gay.*

Wash it away, away. Let Jesus wash it away.
The sin—let Him wash it away. Let's pray.

MENTAL ILLNESS OF A GAY BOY

They changed his chemistry thinking,
It'll help him weather.

He changed his environment, and came out

much better.

SOME QUESTIONS
ABOUT MENTAL ILLNESS

Is mental illness
only from the brain,
or can it be
from outside the body?

Does it only occur
from within the walls of the skull?
Or can it occur
from the walls of the house,
the walls of the state?

Is our mind, our environment,
and our environment, our mind?

—Why does the starry sky
remind me of dreaming?

WORDS TO A SOUTHERN GAY MAN

Embracing your homosexuality, is a sacred thing,
though they say it's not a deep-down thing.

Embracing it—
you won't leap to the opposite because it's expected of you.
You won't push away thoughts of huge hung things,
while the opposite is expected of you.

When time is right, you won't walk down the church aisle,
or you might, and you won't yell and scream because what you truly
    love is naught.

You won't give up your loads to make three kids with some wife,
for elders to tell them why you split.

You won't sling your fist through the drywall,
out of desperation to release yourself from the life you never chose to
    breathe,
but had to breathe in, then abruptly out.

You won't leave your wife cheated and docked like a ship,
because gays can marry now.

All she ever wanted was a husband.
All she ever wanted was love.
All you ever gave her was *sting*—
Two weeks on your knees slurping the neighbor.
Weekends grunting in the garage on someone else's slab.

But really there isn't you to shame,
but the fucked-up society that forced us here.

All you wanted was what you could afford, man on man love,
but they forced you to go after the mansion on the hill.
The tall mansion with pillars designed by them, constructed by them,
    on the hill.

So this is why embracing your homosexuality, is a sacred thing,
though they say it's not a deep-down, domestic thing.

And when these years of misery settle,
while you and your not-wife are on two separate planes,
you'll both look over the land waving at the forced life you despise.
Without having made kids, you two, will stroll on with two separate lives.
Never knowing the singular intricate face of the other—nor that—
the other life when you both were together, suffered.

MEMORIAL DAY

While sipping cold Coke
under strong sun,

while sweat beads
on our foreheads,

seeping through the fence
from the cookout, next door—

"Our soldiers, nowadays,
are a buncha fags, and fairies…"

SOUTHERN-FAGGOT BLUES

after Natasha Trethewey

Just going out to dinner /is a cautious outing.
Just driving out to dinner /is a careful outing.
Holding hands in public /we hear people shouting.

When the neighbors ask who he is /he's always a friend.
When we stand in line at the corner store /we always offend.
Like denial of ourselves /we have to pretend.

Outside our house /we can't express with a flag.
No matter how bad we want /we can't put out our flag.
Our house will be the target: /*the house of the fags.*

We paint on our face /that we don't care.
We keep on that face /but we are aware.
Just the other day /we were cut with glare.

With all this said and done /we feel better off in home.
With all this sad and done /we assume just staying in home.

Safe behind the boards /until the hatery is gone.
Safe behind the boards /until the hatery is gone.

YOU'VE HEARD IT SAID,
NOW HERE'S THE PROOF

Perhaps you can lift your foot
      and put a bandage
         on your toe.

Perhaps you can flip the bird,
      if you want,
    at your hateful neighbor.

Perhaps you can hold your breath
      underwater
        for thirty seconds, if asked.

But one thing you can't control
    is your heart, which is true.

Try to command it,
    right now: *it won't listen.*

VISITING WOLDENBERG PARK

Two dudes prop against railing
next to the Mississippi.

An elder plays the mandolin behind them
under the maples.

A laughing gull flaps
    down, splatting brown-green.

The dudes must be in their late twenties, steaming
under the sun,

shorts and dark hairy legs,
    big glasses,
hair slicked to the side,
    staring over the river
to the Crescent City Connection—far in the blue.

Strolling the sidewalk behind them,
    a gay couple: daiquiris in-hand,
slick legs and dainty—
    stare straight at their butts.

All four men in the blazing sun, hot,
and gazing, "…at that view" I hear one say
"Man!—
Look at that view!"

WHY DON'T CHA?

Oh North, Oh West,
the South is like your ignorant brother
who isn't allowed to go on trips with you.

You should sneak him along some time,
why don't cha?

A THEORY ON SOCIETY

Our house is infested with rats,
      and we have to get a hold of this.
We can't just focus on the rats;
      we have to find the *why*.

We can't just exterminate—
      blow out their stomachs,
hemorrhage under their bones;
      they'll be back. We have to look,

see the slop of dishes we've left behind,
      the pantry floor spattered with corn,
the three bags of trash reeking
      beside the door.

Let's clean it up as much as we can,
      before they gnaw the wires,
set another house,
      the whole neighborhood afire.

THE TRUCKER IS SOCIETY,
THE TREE IS SOCIETY

The trucker glares at his driveway—
how it's saturated, ruined by rain,
how it's nothing but ruts and sludge.

He starts cursing the rain—*it's you
goddamn rain, it's you, fucking rain,*
then hears a *caw* and looks at the tree.

He sees a crow hop a few branches,
then watches a leaf whirl to the ground.
(He doesn't notice the tree-covered
driveway isn't getting any sunlight,
so the absorbent grass can grow.)

And red, pissed-off, yelling at the rain
—*you fucking rain, you goddamn rain*—
never throws a hard word, at the tree.

MINNOWS

The sun beams, beams, beams,
out of the ditch, ditch, ditch,

water evaporates,
evaporates,
evaporates,

the swirl
of minnows,
minnows,

~~minnows~~...

ALL NIGHT THE STORM

bullied and bullied the tree. It pushed
and struck the tree. Until as straight as a stake,

as sharp as a spear, a branch shot
through the roof of the house,

with as much violence as the storm,
which struck the tree, which slung the branch,

which pierced the house.

CAUTION, ANOTHER TRAGIC STORY

Mom, may I dig for crawdads next to Joseph's street?

Of course—as much as you want!

The driver, cutting sharp curve,
suddenly and franticly stung by a wasp, hit the child—

their body flung to the side-brush, as if sleeping...

In the child's last instant, before the hard thump:
They screamed.
The driver screamed. Later,

the mother screamed...

Who's to blame: Driver?... Mother?... Wasp?...

THE WAXING CRESCENT,
LAKE PONTCHARTRAIN
(OR BECAUSE I GOT OFF WORK
AT NINE THIRTY-FIVE)

At the ten-mile marker of the Causeway bridge,
on a February evening, I watch
the huge orange crescent-slice of the moon,
like a perfect boat, off in the west,
the marble-black sky of the west.

I drive, and the bottom of the wedge
illuminated, eases itself
down onto the lake
like a mother dips her child
into water.

For only seconds, you can say,
I'm at the right place at this very time:
I watch the huge orange crescent-slice
of the moon, sail off to another world—

too soon.
too soon.

SOUTHERN SENRYU/HAIKU

At night   across the twenty-four-mile bridge   no streetlights…

A quiet ride home
After a long day's work
Blinker, blinking…

Late at night, reading a book   one cricket:
Chirrrrp.

The barred owl watches the trucker
Roll down the window—

         Toss the can.

He spouts-off a name.

"No worries!"
—Officer rips the ticket.

Thump thump: the raccoon splats the highway…

Two white men prop
On the tailgate of the truck
A faded Trump sticker

A bright cloud floats above the pond—
A dark shadow over water…

"Derik is bullying Keyshawn!"

—*Don't tattle*—
The teacher says.

Two guys on a four-wheeler...

Their friends at home
Can't ever know.

Walking through Walmart
The whole state of Mississippi
On Zoloft.

Tommy,
Randall's friend,
Not Jessica:
Gets the job.

Buying a new iPhone, he laughs—
"I'll look gay!"
The color

The old lady
With five diamonds—
"I don't want help   from a black guy!"

My husband bought our wedding bands.

The receptionist:
"Wow—she did a great job!"

Trash day—
Oops, I did it again!

IV.
How Culture Damns

FIELD CRICKETS

This afternoon, lying in tall grass,
    I hear a chirp, so constant,
        it's almost a hum…

Of course, it's the field crickets.

They're like two cupped palms,
    dipping water to my lips
        after many strenuous miles.

They penetrate the air;
    they pour calm over my body
        like a waterfall.

A peace that almost makes me ask:
    Ah, are you the river?

SOUTHERN LIVING

The field
cricket
rests
under
this   and
long   because
blade   the cricket
of grass,   is under
and so   this   it
does   blade,   lunges
the   chafing   at him
green   his wings   —*snap!*—
anole   to a rhythm
on that   the anole   to preserve
other   does not   itself.
close   understand,
blade,

HOW CULTURE DAMNS

—One—

When you're young
your community says:
the sky will strike down like fangs,
will rip off an appendage
every Thursday,
if from now, until always,
you do not put fresh mint
under your tongue
at 2 a.m.
on Mondays.

Also,
they say: *to succeed in your afterlife,*
every two weeks
you must bury three-fourths of your paycheck
under a doghouse
—and forget it.

—Two—

All your life
you suffer tragic nightmares
about forgetting the mint.

You file bankruptcy
three times before you're forty.

WHAT OPPRESSION WILL DO

Violence is a personal necessity for the oppressed…
It is not a strategy consciously devised.

—Richard Wright

Imagine
you dwell in a steel house
  with no windows.

Imagine
you have eight tabby cats
  and two small dogs
    that you love very much.

Imagine
you have no food.

Imagine
before you leave to get food
  the steel doors *Slam!* then lock.

Imagine
how you're still alive
  five months later…

ANOTHER PROBLEM
WITH SURVIVAL

Oh hawk in the cypress,
you are a crippled old man with dirty nails
who has not eaten in four days
and who begs on the corner of Banks and
Broad. You stand with your hand out, but no one
will offer you a thing.
Every day you lose strength.
Every day you take one street closer.
Then high in the pine bough you see mother-squirrel
move and something pink
drops from her nest.
Oh how you make one frail swoop
and are saved—
tearing and ingesting the eyes, the legs
of her squealing baby.

THE PINK PETUNIA

is full and bright on the patio.

It rains on Wednesday. Then Thursday, then Friday,
it rains. And Saturday and Sunday,
it rains. Monday and Tuesday and Wednesday,
it rains. Through Thursday and Friday,
it rains. Again Saturday and Sunday,
it rains. Until Monday the pink petunia
has wilted

and begins to rot.

THE PAST HAS EVERYTHING
TO DO WITH THE FUTURE

Think of it:
if you don't take the trash to the end of the road,
you're stuck with the reek of crawfish
for another week.

If you don't change the filter,
the A/C will clog and will no longer run.

If you don't feed the dog,
you better bet she'll croak
like a snapper out of water.

The same goes for you and me
and everyone else—

even the snot-nosed kid,
running down the grocery aisle,
poking every boxed cake and bread.

If they are left with an emptiness
—oppressed, rejected,
picked on their entire life,

you better bet when they get older,
they'll fly to every country
under the sun,

will grab at every city
under the sun,

will try and fix it with anything and everything
under the sun.

And if Taiwan doesn't help,
you better bet they'll grab for Paris,

and if Paris doesn't help,
you better bet they'll grab for Rome,

and if Rome doesn't help,
you better bet they'll grab for the bleach,
and eight bottles of pills.

They'll say: "Fuck!
—fuck the booze!"

FELLOW HIKER,

What if we could live in the woods each day?
What if we could soar like a hawk, spread out our wings?
What if we could scurry like a fox?

What if we could cling to the bark, push our way up the oak
to the nest,
or beat our beak into the trunk,
or wind our way to the top and stare out at everything the light
    touches? Yes,
what if we could become everything the light touches?

We aren't of the wild world, not yet.
We are of the human world,

and we must trudge through the muck of our own making,
we must trudge through the thick brush of our own making,
we must push out our arms, to keep the branches from slashing
    our eyes.

Yes, we'll survive. Though it is dark
we mustn't forget the hatchet.

Yes, there are still countless ways—
to cut a path

for the light.

WE, PAST, SPEAK TO YOU, FUTURE

We mumble, like maples mumble in wind.

We open our mouth, like the loon crying,
like the crow's *caw* at the birth of winter.

We say something, send it into the air,
like the pulse of cicadas, near the creek,
or the way the rivers speak. We release our voice
from light-years away, from stardust, like geese
above the fields.

Though our bones have crumbled
into Earth's
sand

that slipped

through our fingers:

We ask, *You*, to endure.
We ask, *You*, to overcome,

what ways we could not.

ABOUT

Ahrend Torrey is the author of *Bird City, American Eye* (Pinyon Publishing, 2022) and *Small Blue Harbor* (Poetry Box Select, 2019). His work has appeared in *storySouth, The Greensboro Review,* and *The Perch* (a journal of the Yale Program for Recovery and Community Health, a program of the Yale School of Medicine), among others. He earned his MA and MFA in creative writing from Wilkes University in Wilkes-Barre, Pennsylvania, and is a recipient of the Etruscan Prize awarded by Etruscan Press. Having lived in the Deep South most all his life, he now lives in Chicago with his husband Jonathan, their two rat terriers Dichter and Dova, and Purl their cat. He is currently working on several new collections of poetry.

www.ingramcontent.com/pod-product-compliance
Lightning Source LLC
Chambersburg PA
CBHW030047100426
42734CB00036B/479